THE LITTLE
BOOK OF

YORKSHIRE

First published in Great Britain 2001 by
Dalesman Publishing Company Limited
Stable Courtyard, Broughton Hall
Skipton, North Yorkshire BD23 3AZ

© Dalesman Publishing Company Limited

A British Cataloguing in Publication record is available for
this book

ISBN 185568 194-3

Cover origination by Grasmere Digital Imaging Limited
Printed by Amadeus Press, Cleckheaton, West Yorkshire

INTRODUCTION

In a bid to pass the time on a train north, a confident southerner announced that he was something of an expert on detecting regional accents even after hearing only the greeting as each passenger had entered the carriage. He went around the three men in the small compartment, pronouncing to the first that he was from Wiltshire and the second from Sunderland. Both nodded impressively. He then turned to the quiet third gent who was staring blankly out of the window and said: "You, my man, are a Lancastrian." The man raised his eyes slowly and replied brusquely: "Nay lad, Ah'm fro' Yorksher – but Ah've been nobbut badly lately."

In this, the smallest book about the biggest county, you'll discover – through some of its traditional sayings and the thoughts of important and influential visitors – just what makes Yorkshire and its people so unique.

See all, hear all, say nowt;
Eat all, sup all, pay nowt,
And if tha ivver does owt for nowt
Do it for thissen.

YORKSHIRE COMMANDMENT

The Yorkshire dalesman is like many of the rivers among which he lives. He is slow but deep and, believe me, it takes years of constant touch with him before one can get into that happy position of being able to read him like a book.

'WONTEN', HAWES (1939)

Here's to thee an' all that's thahn,
Here's to me and all that's mahn.
May all t'good luck that luck
can send
Be thahn and mahn reight up
to t'end
Here's what Ah wish an' what
Ah pray
To leet on all this Christmas Day.

A YORKSHIRE CHRISTMAS WISH

Oft times tha's made me pawn
mi clothes,
Oft times tha's made mi friends
to foes,
But now tha's here afore mi nose,
Up tha pops and dahn tha goes.

TO BE SAID BEFORE DRINKING BEER

Never tell a Yorkshire lass that you're
unworthy of her –
let her find out for herself.

YORKSHIRE FATHER'S ADVICE TO SON

The North is a fat and generous sow lying on her side while the greedy little pigs (the South) feed off her.

GRAHAM TURNER
QUOTING A BATLEY MAN (1967)

Beautiful Swaledale, the land of rest,
Beautiful Swaledale, I love thee
the best.
The land is set in a cultivate style;
The extension of Swaledale is twenty
long mile.

YORKSHIRE BALLAD

Oh Shipley Glen, Oh Shipley Glen,
To Bradford hearts so dear;
The seaside is so far away
But the Salt-aire is always here.

TRADITIONAL RHYME

A heaven so clear, an earth so calm,
So sweet, so soft, so hushed an air,
And deepening still the dream-like
charm
Wild moor-sheep feeding everywhere.

EMILY BRONTE (ON THE MOORS
AROUND HAWORTH)

Here's to you, as good as you are,
Here's to me, as bad as I am,
As bad as I am and as good as you
are,
I'm as good as you, as bad as I am.

YORKSHIRE TOAST

Passions for one's country, yes in the very bones and heart of one, in one's writing, painting, poetry, the songs remembered on a lovely walk, the pictures formed for comfort in ugly places, the memory and tradition and love that makes a network to bind one's heart to the same grey wind-swept upland... My Heart's in Yorkshire.

WINIFRED HOLTBY

A flea will bite whoever it can –
And so my friend will a
Yorkshireman;
A fly will sup with Dick, Tom
or Dan –
And so, begow, will a Yorkshireman!
A magpie can talk for a
terrible span –
And so an' all, can a Yorkshireman;
A flitch is no good till it's hung,
ye'll agree –
No more is a Yorkshireman,
don't ye see.

TRADITIONAL

To Yorkshire cricketers it has become rather more serious than a mere game. It is almost a religion.

TREVOR BAILEY (1961)

Here's to us. May we nivver want owt, none on us, all on us, nor me nawther. Here's health to my wife's husband – tek hod an' sup, lad.

YORKSHIRE TOAST

Birstall for ringers,
Heckmondwike for singers,
Dewsbury for peddlars,
Cleckheaton for sheddlers.

19TH CENTURY COUPLET
(SHEDDLE MEANS TO SWINDLE)

Wharfe is clear and in the Aire lithe,
Where the Aire drowns one, Wharfe
drowns five.

TRADITIONAL

London streets shall run with blood,
And at last shall sink,
So that it shall be fulfill'd
That Lincoln was, London is, and
York shall be
The finest city of the three.

PROPHECY OF NIXON,
THE CHESHIRE MERLIN

For God's sake go easy on the butter.

TRADITIONAL YORKSHIRE GRACE

The Doncaster Mayor he sits
in his chair,
The Mills they merrily go;
His nose doth shine with
drinking wine,
And the gout is in his great toe.
The profits of the town mills were
anciently assigned for special
expenses of the mayor.

TRADITIONAL

I want to go back to Yorkshire and the Wolds, and the smell of tarred ropes and wool, and horses in the dark barns there, and the granaries full of sliding gold and smelling of dust, the sloping field, and slow-speaking shrewd workers.

WINIFRED HOLTBY

I find it difficult to prepare for the constant changes in the weather in the Yorkshire Dales. You awake to a brilliant morning, spend the afternoon sheltering from the tropical downpour and in the evening admire the splendour of the sunset. In New York, you can be 90 per cent sure of the day and dress accordingly.

ALLAN EADY
(AMERICAN VISITOR) 1966

Castleford women must needs be fair,
Because they wash both in Calder
and Aire.

TRADITIONAL

The old people of Hull used to believe that if a husband and wife washed in the same water they would be having a row before they went to bed.

TRADITIONAL

Monday for health,
Tuesday for wealth,
Wednesday the best day of all.
Thursday for losses,
Friday for crosses,
Saturday has no luck at all.

OLD YORKSHIRE SAYING FOR THE
CHOICE OF WEDDING DAY

Never ask a man if he's from Yorkshire. If he is he'll tell you anyway. If he's not you'll only embarrass him.

TRADITIONAL

Them 'at wash on Monday
Have a whole week to dry;
Them 'at wash on Tuesday
Are not so much awry;
Them 'at wash on Wednesday
May get their clothes clean;
Them 'at wash on Thursday
Are not so much so mean;
Them 'at wash on Friday
Wash for their need;
Them 'at wash on Saturday
Are clarty-paps indeed.

TRADITIONAL WASHDAY RHYME

Barnsley… a place famous for all manner of wickedness…

JOHN WESLEY

The Lord be thanked for what
we've getten.
If there'd been more to eat there'd
have been more etten.

YORKSHIRE THANKS

Here's health to thee and thine,
Likewise to me and mine.
When thee and thine come to see me
and mine, me and mine
will try and make thee and thine as
happy as thee and thine made
me and mine when me and mine
come to see thee and thine.

YORKSHIRE THANKS

Harrogate the queerest place, with the strangest people in it, leading the oddest lives.

CHARLES DICKENS (1858)

The rent man was always the most popular chap in Batley – folk were always asking him to call again.

ANON (1953)

The coming of the Lord draweth nigh. Entrance at side door.

SIGN ON A YORKSHIRE CHAPEL

If you have travelled on foot from Hawes to Ingleton you are a walker; and if you have braved the autumn winds tearing over those moorland miles, you are also a wrestler.

LOIS VICTOR COPPIN

Hull, a frightful, dirty, brickhousey, tradesmanlike, rich, vulgar place; yet the river… looked beautiful with the lights upon it, and boats moving about.

DOROTHY WORDSWORTH
(THE GRASMERE JOURNAL, 1802)

One of the charms of the Yorkshire Dales is that they are all characteristically different, like lovely sisters of the same family.

ALFRED J BROWN

Saltburn is select and prettily placed;
Filey quiet, Bridlington bustling; and
Redcar safe...

M J B BADDELEY (1897)

Daftness never built owt worth
leaving up.

YORKSHIRE SAYING

From hence we entered the great county of York, uncertain still which way to begin to take full view of it, for 'tis a county of a very great extent.

DANIEL DEFOE

It's a good hoss that never stumbles
And a good wife that never grumbles.

YORKSHIRE SAYING

When Roseberry Topping
wears a cap
Let Cleveland then beware a clap.

TRADITIONAL

For Angels treat her uplands
And Heaven's about her downs
Her slumbering wolds a-gleaming
With little ancient towns.
From tale enchanted castle
To fairy-haunted glen:
There's witchery in Yorkshire
For Yorkshire-fostered men.

D VIOLET DINSDALE
(SONGS OF YORKSHIRE)

Life in Scarborough is of a very sophisticated, not to say treadmill character. Everybody feeds at the same hours; goes to the spa at the proper times; most do a little fishing and flirting, and wind up with a concert and a dance.

M J B BADDELEY (1897)

The Dales air is like wine, the people generous to a fault, the going good, the views magnificent.

S MAIS

Part of me is still in Bradford, and can never leave it, though when I return there now I wander about half-lost, a melancholy stranger. I am in the right place but not at the right time. But in the world outside… something at the core of me is still in Market Street hearing the Town Hall chimes.

J B PRIESTLEY (1962)

Hard work's killed nobody – but
thowt on it's killed many a thousand.

ESKDALE PEAT CUTTER

T'belly keeps t'back up. You can't
work without some packing.

BIG BILL, SWALEDALE

There are things they do at Buckden,
At Arncliffe and Aptrick, too,
That we who live in Burnsall
Would rather die than do.
With Grassington's behaviour
We don't see eye to eye,
for the moral tone of Burnsall
Is very, very high.

TRADITIONAL

What do you think of Yorkshire
Pudding, I'm frequently asked. Well,
I've eaten this half a dozen times,
and it has been a different shape, size
and colour each time. I've had it
with, without, under and above
gravy, with and without meat. I am
extremely confused. The whole thing
is too mysterious.

ALLAN EADY
(AMERICAN VISITOR) 1966

Them as eats most pudding gets most meat.

A REFERENCE TO THE CANNY YORKSHIRE PRACTICE OF SERVING YORKSHIRE PUDDINGS FIRST TO FILL UP DINERS BEFORE THE EXPENSIVE MEAT COURSE

Tha thi's them as thi's thee.

SOUND ADVICE ON WHEN TO USE THE
FAMILIAR THEE

So pre-eminent in size over all the rest of the counties of England as to merit its name of the Land of Broad Acres, its boundries marked for the most part by mountain stream and ocean, Yorkshire presents within itself perhaps the most complete epitome of physical geography and geological study to be found in any other equal area on the globe.

M TAIT

I was always very proud of living in Yorkshire, in that hilly part which is called the backbone of England, the Pennine Chain… at night I loved to see the lighted trams climbing up the dark hills like fireflies on black velvet; it seemed to me that they were brave and sturdy, like Yorkshire people, not afraid of difficult tasks or big hills.

PHYLLIS BENTLEY

I toured the Pennines on foot in wind, slush and sleet, for the benefit of my heart.

R A SCOTT MACFIE (1917)

Be wary, be chary,
Tek heed who tha courts.
There's lasses a plenty,
All sizes an' sorts;
But if tha's to be happy,
Tek on wi' a lass
'At's nimble wi t'thimble
An' careful wi t'brass.

THE WEAVER TO HIS SON

Never buy owt wi' a wooden handle
– it allus means hard work.

YORKSHIRE PROVERB

I rode over the mountains to Huddersfield. A wilder people I never saw in England; the men, women and children filled the streets as we rode along, and appeared just ready to devour us.

FROM THE DIARIES OF JOHN WESLEY

The Yorkshireman has many of the qualities of the moors on which, or on whose edges he dwells. He is often harsh, gnarled, prickly; tenacious of his rights and only roughly picturesque...

W RILEY (A YORKSHIRE SUBURB, 1920)

It is in most places waste, solitary, unpleasant, unsightly, mute and still... especially about the head of the River Ure, which having a bridge over it of one entire stone, falleth down such a depth that it striketh a certain horror to as many as look down.

WILLIAM CAMDEN (ON THE SOURCE OF THE RIVER URE, 1590)

Yorkshire is a kingdom in miniature, with five universities, five cathedrals, mountains, moors, potholes, slag heaps, smoke and fumes and a lot of catarrh.

BISHOP ERIC TREACY

Bradford for cash,
Halifax for dash,
Wakefield for pride and poverty;
Huddersfield for show,
Sheffield what's low,
Leeds for dirt and vulgarity.

A R WRIGHT
(ENGLISH FOLK-LORE, 1928)

He's a strong, silent type. Bears no grudges and little malice. But he can be irritating and pig headed; often unbearably old fashioned, especially where money is concerned, and spares little for what he calls extravagances (especially clothes for me and the children). Although he rarely shows emotion I know he cares greatly for us and works day and night to keep us comfortable.

FROM A YORKSHIRE HOUSEWIFE'S DAIRY (LATE 19TH CENTURY)

Thence to Hardraw, where's hard hunger,
Barren cliffs and clints (ravines) of wonder...
Inns are nasty, dusty, fusty,
With both smoke and rubbish musty.

RICHARD BRAITHWAITE (1648)

Yorkshiremen are suspicious, obstinate, materialist, isolationist, nonconformist and blunt – and I like them as they are.

BISHOP ERIC TREACY

...but he (the Yorkshireman) has many characteristics that are admirable and distinctly English: he has a dogged perseverance, great strength of will, sound judgement, ready wit. And withal he has a heart that is very tender.

W RILEY
(A YORKSHIRE SUBURB, 1920)

(Prior to reorganisation in 1974)
Yorkshire boasted an acreage of
3,923,359 – more acres than there are
letters in the Bible.

TRADITIONAL

'Pity poor Bradford'

A GHOST AT BOLLING HALL, BRADFORD

One trouble is that every Yorkshire person has several layers of speech. He won't talk quite the same to the vicar, to a baby, and to a workmate who drops a paving slab on his toe!

PETER WRIGHT
(DIALECT EXPERT)

If Whitby fishermen see a pig on the way to their boats, they believe it to be so unlucky they won't put to sea.

TRADITIONAL

When William Sharp of Laycock near Keighley was rejected by a local barmaid he went home to bed and stayed there until he died – 49 years later (of cramp).

DALESMAN

I like my fellow men but there are times when it is wonderful to be utterly alone in a wide landscape. There aren't many places in England where you can do this, but you can do it in my Yorkshire.

'JAMES HERRIOT'

To safeguard his flour from theft he would press his face into the flour at the top of the bin, and then put his face back into the impression on returning.

SAID OF OLD JOHN MEALY FACE OF TOPCLIFFE (EARLY 1800s)

…the history of York is the history of England…

KING GEORGE V

The Dales have never disappointed me. I still consider them the finest countryside in Britain, with their magnificent, clean and austere outlines of hill and moor, their charming villages and remote whitewashed farms, their astonishing variety of aspect and appeal, from the high gaunt rocks down to the twinkling rivers.

J B PRIESTLEY

Sutton, boiled mutton,
    Brotherton beef,
Ferrybridge bonny lass
And Knottingley thief.

OLD SAYING

You can allus tell a Yorkshireman –
but you can't tell him much.

TRADITIONAL

From Hell, Hull and Halifax, Good
Lord deliver us!

THIEVES' LITANY REFERRING TO THE
HALIFAX GIBBET — A GUILLOTINE-LIKE
PUNISHMENT FOR ROGUES

The Yorkshireman's coats of arms include a fly and a flea (to represent sponging and backbiting) and a flitch of bacon (because Yorkshiremen and bacon are both said to be better for hanging).

TRADITIONAL

Yan, tan,
tethera, methera,
pip,
teaser, leaser,
catra, horna,
dick

TRADITIONAL SHEPHERD'S NUMERALS
FOR COUNTING SHEEP

Yorkshire folk seem to be the most individual and diverse I have yet met. Sometimes it is a little nerve-racking to face their positive and, if I may be forgiven, almost blunt approach; but at the end of an interview you are left in little doubt of their opinion. This is encouraging when you think you have made a good impression and discouraging when you know you haven't.

ALLAN EADY
(AMERICAN VISITOR) 1966

Far to the North, where bold
Brigantine Kings ruled aweful, ere
the martial clime was hailed by the
loved name of York.

ANON. (1809)

This yah neet, this yah neet,
Ivery neet an' all.
Fire an' fleet an' cann'l leet,
An' Christ tak up thi sawl.

LYKE WAKE DIRGE, CHANTED BY
WALKERS ON THE 40-MILE CROSSING
OF THE LYKE WAKE WALK ON THE
NORTH YORK MOORS

It's absolutely impossible for any of us, no matter how fond we may be of our native county, to comprehend its vast size. Folks who live outside the borders cannot form any conception of its enormous area, of the difference between its three Ridings, of the alternations in scenery, of the gulf which separates the men of its towns and cities from men of the lovely dales and woodlands.

J S FLETCHER

God bless us all and mek us able
Ta eyt all t'stuff 'ats on this table.

ROBUST YORKSHIRE GRACE

The rocks on each side, which joining with the side of the cave, formed the vista of the brook, were chequered with three dimunitive waterfalls or rather courses of water. Each of theses was a minature of all that summer and winter can produce of delicate beauty.

WORDSWORTH (LETTER TO COLERIDGE ON HARDRAW FORCE)

Invention hence her compass steers towards York, the most renowned of shires, makes the three Ridings in their stories each severally to show their glories.

M DRAYTON

Grouse calling, and the smell of t' mistal are in my original list of pleasures remembered. Your bed of heather and bracken is a grand flashback for me to Ilkley Moor and over to Blubberhouses.

JOHN DOWER

If Yorkshire were in the field, there was the thrill of watching the perfect machine in action; brilliant bowling, backed up by superb fielding… And they are all united here in one common purpose, to play the game and uphold the honour of the White Rose, and to put Yorkshire firmly and squarely at the top of the championship table.

ALFRED J BROWN – FROM 'BROAD ACRES'

My girl's a Yorkshire girl,
Yorkshire through and through.
My girl's a Yorkshire girl,
Eh! by gum but she's a champion!
Though she's a factory lass
And wears no fancy clothes.
I've a sort of a Yorkshire relish
For my little Yorkshire rose!

PANTOMIME SONG (1909)

She's just a lass from Yorkshire
A little country maiden,
With eyes of blue, that all day
through are laughter laden.
Until the day I met her
My heart was fancy free.
But oh! my little Yorkshire lassie
You are the girl for me!

FROM 'OUR MISS GIBBS'

Amongst the mountains high of Craven, where blue heads for caps put on the sky.

M DRAYTON

Nine months of winter and three months of backend!

A LOCAL'S SOUR REFLECTION ON SWALEDALE'S CLIMATE

Take the isolated farms that appeared to be part of the hills on which they were pitched, slopes that swept down to streams below, with the particular beauty of the Yorkshire countryside… having a distant, sad, pure beauty that breathes the air of perpetual childhood.

OSBERT SITWELL
(FROM 'THE SCARLETT TREE')

Where there's muck there's brass.

MUCH QUOTED ADAGE ON THE
WEALTH OF YORKSHIRE'S BOOMING
INDUSTRIAL TOWNS

There is no air more pure
Than the thin dome of crystal
that enskies
Those Pennine fells, with blue
faint as the eyes
Of wan forget-me-nots.

FRANCIS BRETT YOUNG

To begin wi' a Yorkshire pudding is eaten by itsen and not mixed up wi' meat and potaters, all in a mush. And it comes straight out o' t' oven... No waiting, or you'll spoil it. If you don't put it straight on to t' plate you might as well go and sole your boots with it.... If you've mixed right an' your oven's hot, pudding'll come out as light as a feather, crisp an' brahn, just a top and a bottom, you might say, wi' none o' this custardy stuff in t' middle.

JESS OAKROYD OF BRUDDERSFORD
(BRADFORD) IN J B PRIESTLEY'S
'GOOD COMPANIONS'

Never, as long as I live, will I forget the shuddering awe that possessed me as I stood, one chilly and gloomy afternoon in the savage gorge of Gordale Skar *(sic)*, my cheek wet with the spray from torrent that thundered, foaming down from rock precipice, frowning six hundred feet above my head.

THOMAS GRAY

Welcome, my lord, to this brave town of York!

SHAKESPEARE (HENRY VI)

Yorke, Yorke, for my monie,
Of all the cities that ever I see, for
merry pastime and companie.

OLD BALLARD (1580)

Our ancient and loyal City of York has always been famous for keeping up a hearty and neighbourly way among ourselves, which keeps us all friends.

TRADITIONAL PLAY (1716)

At York in the evening, I spoke to the far genteelest audience I have had since I left Edinburgh.

JOHN WESLEY

I had like to have lost my heart at York. It is a terrible thing to have such a place in the Church as I have; nothing but ladies by dozens, and very pretty ones, on the right hand and the left or in front of my stall. But through mercy, having the service to read, I was forced to look at least as much upon the rubrick of the book, as upon that of their cheeks. So I am returned safe and sound!

E PYLE (1751)

Ask an East Riding man where to find the real Yorkshire, and he will take you straight to the Wolds… And truly it is in the Wolds that one derives perhaps the best impression of a land of broad acres, for from any of the gentle ridges one looks over immense vistas of undulating arable land, acres of corn and green pastures.

ALFRED J BROWN

...nor is the town of Hull itself to be overlooked. It is a little city of London; streets, shops, everything like it; clean as the best parts of London and the people as bustling and attentive.

WILLIAM COBBETT

Whitby stands superbly and masterly above the sea, looking out to the rolling ocean, over which a Yorkshire boy was to sail away to find a continent, and to give security to the British Empire by making life safe in our ships.

ARTHUR MEE (ON CAPTAIN COOK)

If you had early come under the spell of this immensity of mountains, and the vastness of sweeping moorland, say when these are the heritage of man or woman, he or she, like a homing pigeon, never forgets, and never loses the urge to return to that spiritual home; where is a combination of grandeur, peace, poetry, music and abiding content.

J FAIRFAX BLAKEBOROUGH
ON YORKSHIRE

One of the charms of the Yorkshire Dales is that they are all characteristically different, like lovely sisters of the same family. Each Dale has its distinctive features, folklore and legends, and each must be explored from end to end if one wishes to understand its fame and beauty.

ALFRED J BROWN

If you want variety, start from Richmond and explore the castles and abbeys in the Yorkshire Dales. The air up here is like wine, the people generous to a fault, the going good, the views magnificent…

S P B MAIS

Wakefield is a clean, large, well built town, very populous and very rich; here is a very large church, and well filled, it is; the steeple is a very fine spire. Here also is a market every Friday for woolen cloathes *(sic)* after the manner of that at Leeds.

DANIEL DEFOE

No writer of novels could make a picture of Yorkshire life half as full of meaning as the one drama every year in [cricket] matches between Lancashire and Yorkshire.

NEVILLE CARDUS

In a few years, it was common saying that there were three strange wants at Wakefield: a parson wanting pride, young men wanting wives, and ale-houses wanting customers.

GOLDSMITH

The joke about Yorkshire Cricket is that for Yorkshiremen it is no laughing matter. It is a possession of the clan, and must on no account be put down or interfered with by anybody not born in the County…

NEVILLE CARDUS

The hoary rocks, the falling towers,
The stately dome and shady bowers,
The verdant fields and pendant wood
On Nidd's meandering silver flood.

ANON (EARLY 19TH CENTURY – ON
KNARESBOROUGH)

Her greatest and chiefest town, the name that doth derive From Don's near bordering banks.

M DRAYTON (ON DONCASTER)

I dreamt last night of England
and the rain,
grey clouds across the Yorkshire hills,
and mist
haunting the moors, curled low
in every grain;
close-huddled sheep keeping
bedraggled tryst

behind a broken wall; smell of wet
heather;
music of rushing streams;
beat of the wind;
one solitary shepherd… "Mucky
weather!"…
"Aye, dampish… an' ah've three
young lambs to find."

WILLIAM COWLEY

Wheer they put t'pigs on t'wall to
listen to t'band.

SAID OF MARSDEN

Slow-wit, wheer they raked t'mooin
aht o' t'cut.

SAID OF SLAITHWAITE

Halifax is built of wax
Heptonstall of stooan
I' Halifax there's bonny lasses
I' Heptonstall there's nooan.

TRADITIONAL

When all the world shall be aloft,
then Hallamshire shall be God's
croft.

TRADITIONAL

They are a race powerful both in mind and body.

MRS GASKELL ON YORKSHIRE FOLK